Making Their Mark: Women In Sports™

Kristi Yamaguchi
World-Class Ice Skater

Liza N. Burby

The Rosen Publishing Group's

PowerKids Press™
New York

Published in 1997 by The Rosen Publishing Group, Inc.
29 East 21st Street, New York, NY 10010

First Edition

Book Design: Erin McKenna

Photo Credits: Cover and pp. 4, 8, 11, 12, 15, 16, 19, 20 © AP/Wide World Photos, Inc.; p. 7 © John Terence Turner/FPG International Corp.

Burby, Liza N.
    Kristi Yamaguchi / by Liza N. Burby
        p.   cm. — (Making their mark, women in sports)
    Includes index.
    Summary: Covers the life and achievements of the Olympic champion figure skater Kristi Yamaguchi.
    ISBN 0-8239-5065-4 (lib. bdg.)
    1. Yamaguchi, Kristi—Juvenile literature. 2. Skaters—United States—Biography—Juvenile literature.
    3. Women skaters—United States—Biography—Juvenile literature. [1. Yamaguchi, Kristi. 2. Ice skaters.
    3. Japanese Americans—Biography. 4. Women—Biography.] I. Title. II. Series: Burby, Liza N. Making
their mark.
    GV850.Y36B87 1997
    796.91'092—dc21
    [B]   96–53334
                                                          CIP
                                                            AC

Manufactured in the United States of America

Contents

Kristi Has a Dream

Kristi Yamaguchi was born on July 12, 1971, in Hayward, California. Kristi was just five years old when she watched **figure skater** (FIG-yer SKAY-ter) Dorothy Hamill win a gold medal in the 1976 Olympics. From that moment on, Kristi wanted more than anything to be like Dorothy. Kristi decided she was going to be a skater. This was a big dream for someone who was born with club feet. This meant that her feet were not straight. When Kristi was a little girl, she wore casts on her feet to straighten them out.

◀ Kristi always dreamed of being a world-class skater.

5

A Young Girl on Ice

When Kristi was six, she begged her mother to let her try ice skating. Her mother thought this would be good exercise for Kristi's legs and feet. She said yes. Kristi's mother had no idea how much her little girl would love to skate. Soon, Kristi was taking lessons twice a week. After a lot of hard work, she learned how to spin and jump on the ice. She also learned that every skater falls.

Like this little girl, many girls take skating lessons in hopes of becoming Olympic skaters. ▶

A Hard Schedule

Kristi was small for her age, but she was very strong. When she was nine, her parents decided that Kristi was good enough to have her own skating teacher. Kristi began working with a teacher named Christy Kjarsgaard. Kristi had a hard **schedule** (SKED-yul). She woke up at 4:00 a.m. four days a week in order to get to the skating rink by 5:00 a.m. for practice. She skated for five hours and then went to school.

◀ Kristi works with other young skaters to help them work toward their dreams.

9

Hard Work

In 1983, Kristi began skating with a partner, thirteen-year-old Rudi Galindo. They worked with a coach named Jim Hulick. Now Kristi had to practice even more hours on the ice. She still worked with Christy in the mornings before school. Then she spent every afternoon skating with Rudi. All this practicing didn't leave much time for Kristi to make friends at school. But she didn't seem to mind—as long as she could skate.

As long as she could skate, Kristi didn't care about the many hours of practice. ▶

Kristi and Rudi Win a Contest

In 1985, Kristi and Rudi skated so well together that they entered a **national** (NAH-shun-ul) contest for **junior** (JOON-yer) skaters. They won fifth place at the U.S. Nationals junior pairs competition. Judges liked their skating so much that they asked Kristi and Rudi to **compete** (kum-PEET) in the World Championships in Yugoslavia. The partners skated well and scored fifth place again. They were the fifth best pairs team in the world. But Kristi wasn't happy with being fifth. She wanted to be number one.

◄ On and off the ice, Kristi was determined to be one of the best skaters in the world.

Two Titles for Kristi

Right after Kristi turned sixteen, she and Rudi **qualified** (KWAL-ih-fyd) to skate in the World Championships again. This time Kristi wanted to win two **titles** (TY-tulz). She skated alone in the **singles** (SIN-gulz) competition and she won first place. Then she and Rudi skated together. They won the junior title. Kristi's hard work had paid off. That year, Kristi was named the Up-and-Coming Artistic Athlete of the Year by the Women's Sports Foundation.

Kristi is seen by many organizations as a role model. ▶

An Artist on Ice

In 1989, Kristi and Rudi won their first **senior** (SEEN-yer) title, a gold medal in the pairs competition at the National Championships. Kristi also won second place in the singles event. This made her the first woman in 35 years to win two medals at the championships. Sportswriters really liked Kristi's skating. They wrote that her skating was artistic and beautiful. The 5-foot, 93-pound girl twirled and leaped and danced on the ice. Her skating was exciting to watch.

◀ Kristi's style of artistic skating is known around the world.

17

Hard Decisions

When Kristi finished high school, her life began to change. Her singles coach, Christy, married and moved to Canada. Kristi went too. It was the first time she had lived away from her family. Then Jim, her pairs coach, died of cancer. That year, Kristi made some hard decisions. She decided she could not skate both singles and in pairs as well as she wanted. She chose singles. She and Rudi stopped skating together.

Despite some big life changes, Kristi ▶ remains dedicated to her skating.

Dreams of Gold Come True

By 1990, Kristi was among the top four skaters in the world. She won another gold medal at the 1992 National Championships. This made her able to skate in the 1992 Winter Olympics in Lillehammer. She fell once during the Olympic competition. But Kristi skated so well that she won the gold medal anyway. She became the first American to win the gold since her hero, Dorothy Hamill, won it in 1976. Kristi had dreamed of becoming an Olympic champion. Her dream had come true.

◀ Hard work and dedication have helped Kristi to be one of the best figure skaters in the world.

A Belief in Herself

After she won the gold medal in the Olympics, Kristi became a very famous young woman. She starred in TV commercials, and was on cereal boxes and magazine covers. Today, she skates in ice shows around the world, showing people how much happiness skating has brought to her life. She likes to tell people that whatever their dream is, they have to believe in themselves. Then they have to work hard to make that dream come true. And Kristi has always done just that.

Glossary

compete (kum-PEET) To try hard to win something.

figure skater (FIG-yer SKAY-ter) A person who jumps, spins, and dances on ice.

junior (JOON-yer) A skater who competes in young adult skating events.

national (NAH-shun-ul) An event that takes place in one's own country.

qualified (KWAL-ih-fyd) To be ready to do something.

schedule (SKED-yul) A plan of what one has to do at certain times.

senior (SEEN-yer) A skater who competes in adult skating events.

single (SIN-gul) Only one person or thing.

title (TY-tul) Top award.

23

Index